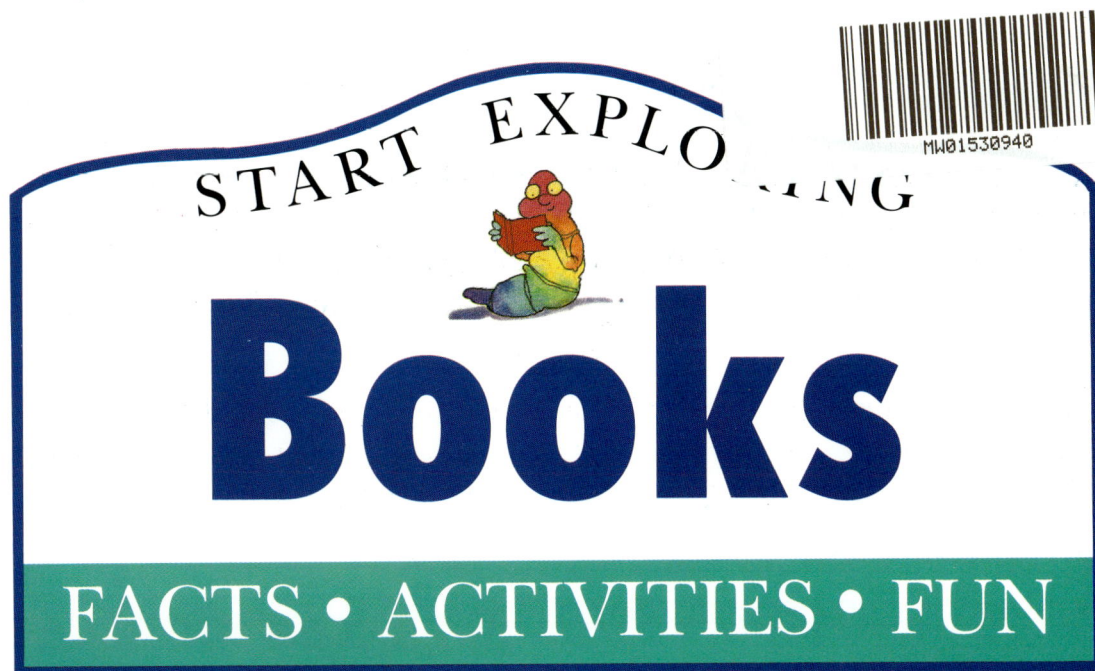

START EXPLORING

Books

FACTS • ACTIVITIES • FUN

Alison Boyle

Illustrated by Sascha Lipscomb

A Alexandre

CONTENTS

Headway · Hodder & Stoughton

Who's who?

A book begins in someone's head. This is not as uncomfortable as it sounds. It's the idea for the book really!

Then there is a lot of talking and testing and, if all the people at the publishing company agree, the book is made.

A lot of people are involved in making books. Here are some of them.

I'm the author. I write the book. I write at home.

I'm the editor. I decide which books we want to publish, and find authors to write them.

I'm the desk editor. I suggest changes to be made to the book, and check the proofs. I work with the designer.

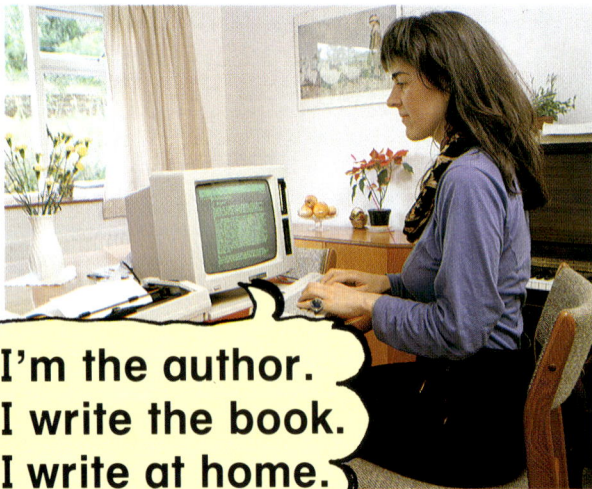

Psst...if you haven't already guessed I'm a bookworm and I love books. I hope you will try all the booky puzzles and activities along the way - they really are delicious.

I'm the designer. I decide what the book will look like. I choose the typeface the book will be printed in.

I'm in publicity. I tell everybody I can about the new books so they will want to read them.

I'm a sales rep. I sell the books to shops where you buy them.

I'm in production. I choose which paper to use for the book and arrange for it to be printed.

AMAZING FACTS!

Books can be cheap or expensive. A book is cheaper if

- it has only a few pages.

- it is printed in 1 or 2 colours. Most books are printed in 1 colour (black) or 4 colours (black, red, yellow and blue).

- the pages are stapled or stuck rather than sewn.

Words

The editor and author talk about what the book should have in it. The author then writes a book plan.

When the editor has read the plan she has a meeting with the sales and marketing department. They talk about how much making the book will cost. They want to make sure that people will want to buy the book.

AMAZING FACTS!

Enid Blyton wrote 700 children's books in her lifetime. She wrote 59 of these in 1 year (1955)!

The rights manager then contacts publishers around the world to translate the book into other languages. Some books are sold in over 50 different languages.

Z • ? P Q S

The author then writes the book. Some authors use word processors and send a disc to the editor. This can be slotted into the computers at the publishing company.

The disc remembers all the information.

Now You See

Pretend you are an author and think of a good story for a book.

- Who will be in the story?
- How will the story start?
- What will happen?

The desk editor checks that everything has been spelt properly and that it all makes sense.

Pictures

The author makes a list of the pictures she would like in the book.

The designer works out how the words and pictures will appear on each page. He makes sketches on paper or plans it out using a computer to see how much space there will be for the pictures.

Then he asks an illustrator to draw the pictures. The illustrator draws pictures following the designer's instructions about style. Should the pictures be serious or funny, in colour or black and white?

If a book has photographs in it the designer asks a photographer to take them.

Or the designer borrows the photographs from a special **photo library** which lends out photographs for money.

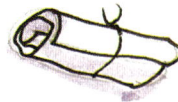

The bromide is stuck on to big pieces of card and photocopies of the photographs are stuck on a piece of tracing paper over the top to show the printer the exact position of the words and pictures.

Meanwhile, the words have been keyed into a special machine called a **typesetting machine** and printed out on to a very high quality paper called **bromide**. A photograph can be taken of this to make the printing plate.

Now You See

Think of the story you made up on page 5.

- Pretend you are a designer. Decide what the pages are going to look like.

- Then be an illustrator and draw pictures to go on to the pages.

Colours

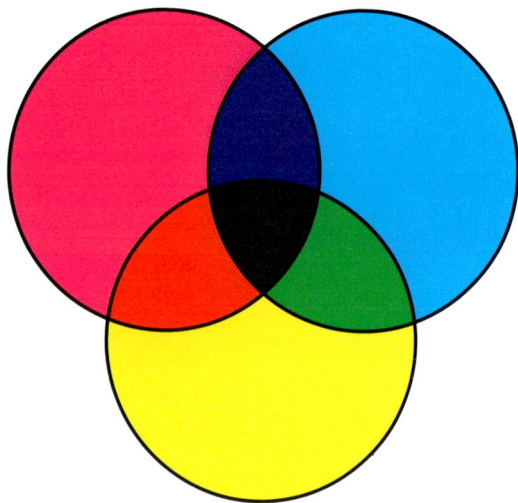

All the colours we see in books are a mixture of the same three colours - red, blue and yellow. Red is called **magenta**, blue **cyan**, and yellow **yellow**!

What happens if you mix these colours? Try mixing paint to see.

cyan + yellow

magenta + yellow

magenta + cyan

At the reproduction company, the pictures are put on a machine called a **scanner**. Its computer reads how much of each colour - magenta, cyan and yellow, is in each part of the pictures.

Pictures aren't printed as solid blocks of colour. They are made up of lots of tiny dots. The more dots there are and the smaller they are, the better you will be able to see the picture when it is printed.

This is a scanning machine.

Which cat is easiest to see?

The one on the left! This is because there are more smaller dots packed into the same space.

The words and pictures are put together on film. These same images are then made on metal printing plates. Everything is printed on large sheets of paper called proofs, or on a thick plastic called a **Cromalin**.

Checking

The desk editor, designer and production person check the proofs for mistakes. They make sure that the colours match the original pictures.

They use a small magnifying glass to see things more clearly. Changes are written or drawn on the proof.

Now You See

Ask a grown-up if they have a magnifying glass.

If you look through the glass at any colour picture in a book or magazine, you should be able to see the dots used to print the picture.

The editor checks for mistakes. Can you find any in these sentences?

Eloise throw the boll and it went flying ver the fence. Now she wuld have to tel her dod.

The proofs with the changes are sent back to the factory.

yellow

magenta

yellow + magenta

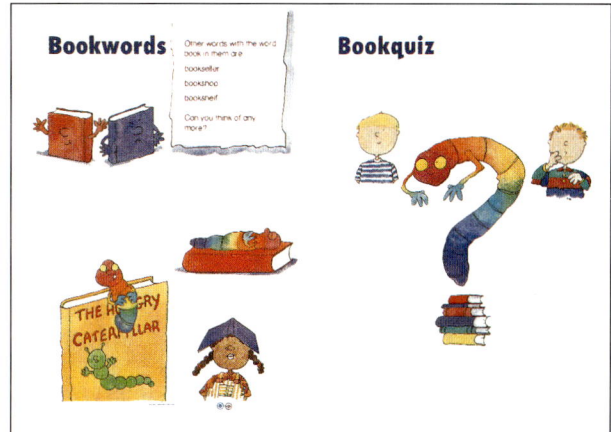

yellow + magenta + cyan

Four sheets of correct film are made for each page - one each for black, magenta, cyan and yellow. What are their more common names?

The film is then sent back for the editor, designer and production person to check that all the changes have been made. And then the film is sent to the printing company…phew!

Black and yellow are easy peasy!

11

Your book

Now it's your turn to make a book!
Decide what your book will be about.
In the middle of this book there is a piece of card. This is your book cover.
Ask a grown-up to open the staples, to pull out the card, then close the staples again.

Fill in the boxes with photographs or pictures. Colour your cover.

The first page is the front cover.

Write the title at the top and the author - this is you!

The last page is the back cover. Write down some of the best things in the book.

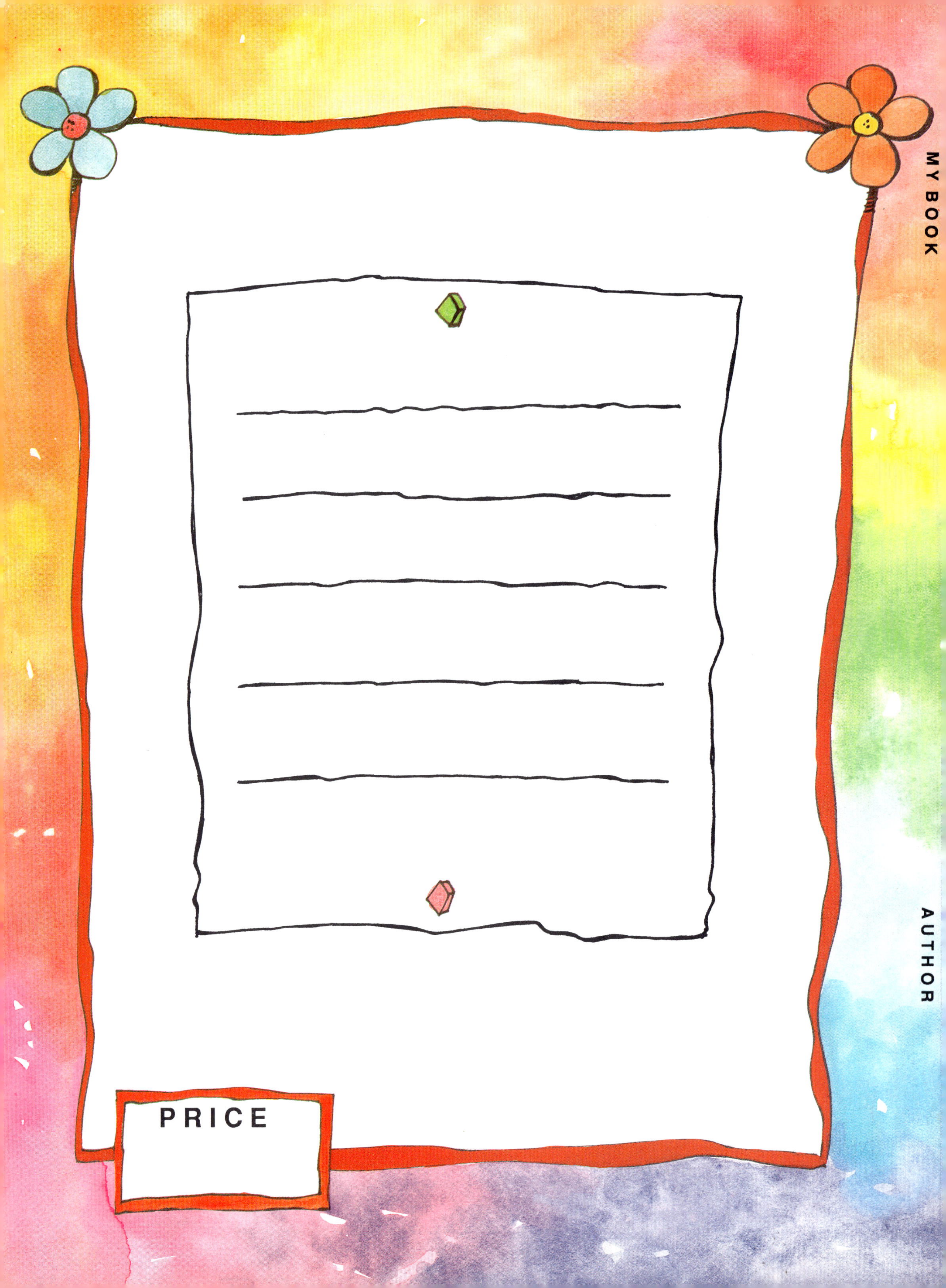
MY BOOK
AUTHOR
PRICE

MY BOOK

_____

_____

AUTHOR

Ask a grown-up to help you cut out 10 sheets of paper the same depth as your cover but twice as wide. You can use coloured paper if you like.

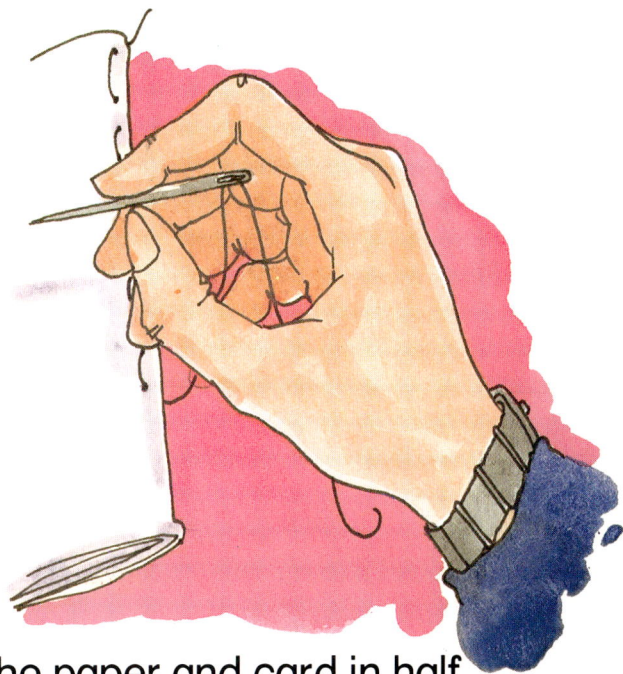

Fold the paper and card in half. Ask a grown-up to help you sew the pages together with a thick thread and needle. Remember to knot the ends.

Here is my story book

Now you are ready to write your book.

Add pictures as you go along.

Printing

The printer uses the film to make metal printing plates. These plates are wrapped round the huge rollers of the printing machine.

The type of printing machine used depends on how many books are to be made.

For bigger jobs, this type of machine might be used.

The paper is pulled through the machine and printed on one side. Then it is pulled through again upside-down so that the other side can be printed.

For small jobs, this type of machine might be used.

The printer checks the first sheets that come off the press to make sure that the colours are right. More ink may be allowed to flow on to the paper, or less, to correct the colours.

The printed sheets have to be as close to the original proofs as possible - this is what the publishing company is expecting.

Usually the cover is printed on thicker, shinier paper, so that it doesn't wear out too quickly when people are using the book.

AMAZING FACTS!

Most people think that the oldest book ever printed was the **Gutenberg Bible**. This was in Germany in 1454.

There may be an older book, though. This contains poetry from the Tang Dynasty, dated 1160 - almost 3,000 years earlier!

The biggest book ever printed was **The Super Book**, in the USA. It was 2.74 x 3.07 metres.

The smallest book was **Old King Cole!**, published in Scotland in 1985. The pages can only be turned with a needle.

Binding

The printed sheets of paper are folded, cut, then sorted into the right order. This is called **collating.**

If they were put in the wrong order, you wouldn't be able to read the book properly.

The pages of your book have been stapled together with big, strong wires.

A factory can sew, staple or glue the spine of a book to keep the pages together.

Books can have soft covers (paperback books), or hard covers (hardback books). A cover protects the pages of a book from being damaged while it is being read.

The covers are put on last.

Now You See

Pick up any storybook and read the last page first. Then go back to the first page. Then skip a few pages. It doesn't make sense, does it?

Make up a story where the events are all jumbled. Then tell it to someone you know. At the end, ask them to work out the right order. It's probably more difficult than they think!

Packing

The bound books are stacked inside the warehouse in big piles on top of wooden blocks called pallets.

Can you guess why the wooden blocks have holes?

The metal prongs at the front of the fork-lift truck are moved inside the holes of the pallets. The books are then carried to a place from where they can be sent out.

other countries

The books are sent from the warehouse to many places.

bookshops

Bo
War

newsagents

library suppliers

The sales representative, who works for the publishing company, has sold books to as many bookshops as she can.

museums

book club warehouses

OK
house

school book fairs

supermarkets

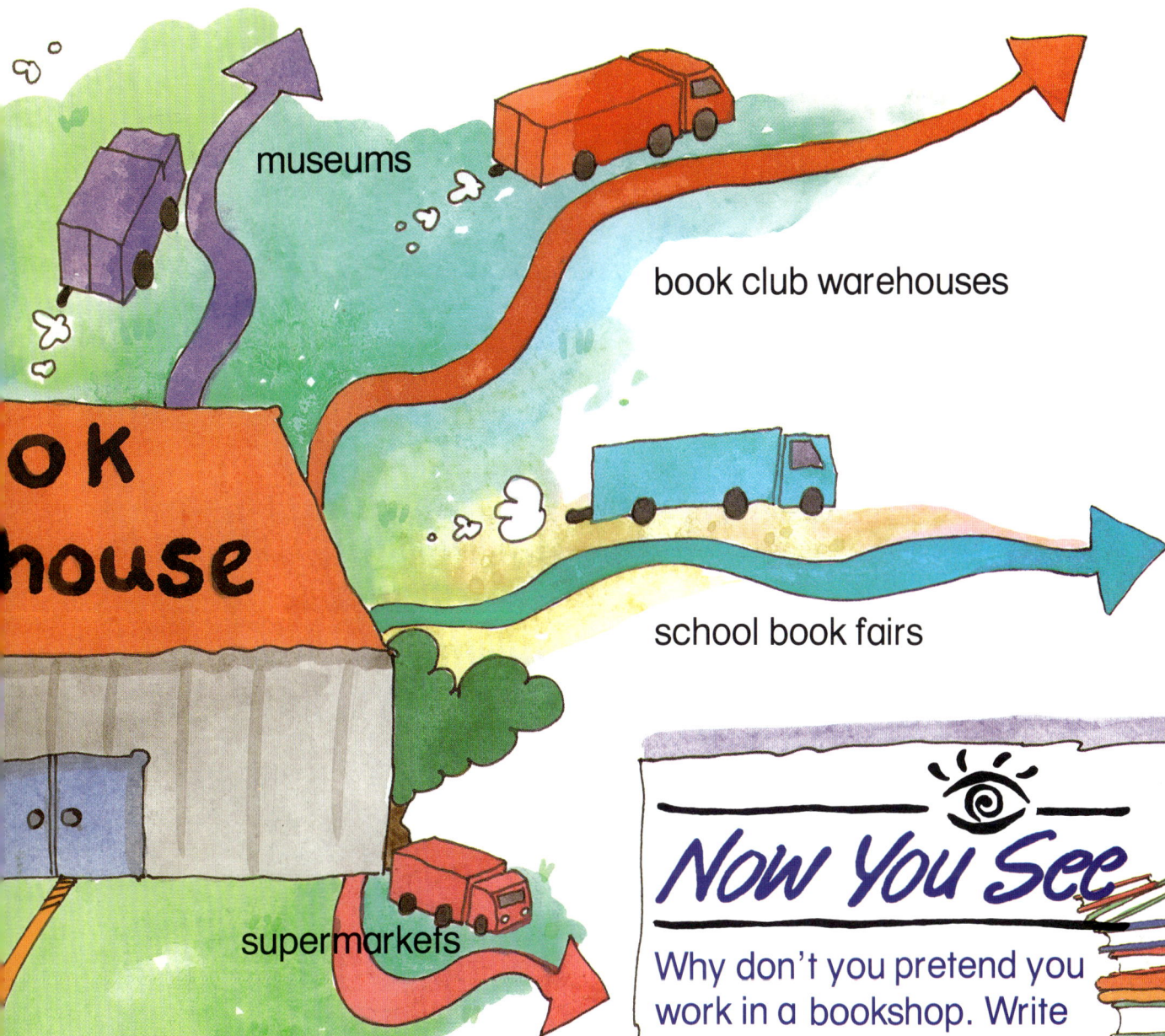

The order says how many of this book each shop wants. The right number of books is packed with an address label.

```
25x        Ms Betty Blue
BOOKS      The Big Bookshop
           Biggin Hill
           Baggythorpe
Order      BOLTON
Number     Lancashire
KT@@£      BB128BB
```

Now You See

Why don't you pretend you work in a bookshop. Write out your own orders for books - ask for your favourites!

Bookshops

In a bookshop the books are usually arranged in different sections such as novels, travel books, cookery books and children's books. This makes it easy for you to find what you want to buy.

Sometimes books are displayed in a special pack called a dumpbin which helps catch people's attention and maybe persuades them to buy a copy.

Not all books produced are sold. If the bookshop does not sell a book it can return it to the publishing company and get its money back.

AMAZING FACTS!

Barbara Cartland, who writes romantic books, has sold over 500 million copies of her 516 titles.

Libraries

Books in libraries are also arranged in different sections such as stories, information books, maps, tapes and cassettes, and books with large writing that are used by people whose eyes don't see very well. There is usually a children's section with bright chairs, cushions and book boxes.

You can normally borrow books and take them home to read for 3 weeks.

If you don't bring the books back on time you might have to pay a fine!

Some books can only be read in the library. These are reference books such as dictionaries and encyclopedias.

Bookwords

To be in someone's good (or bad) books means you are liked (or not liked) by them.

Other words with the word book in them are...

bookseller

bookshop

bookshelf

Can you think of any more?

b o o k a n t i c s

Play this game with friends. One of you makes up a word, and the others describe what it means. For example,

BOOK BED

You could be called a bookworm, too, if you like reading. It's a bit like saying, "She always has her head in a book." That's what a bookworm like me is doing - nibbling away. Little rotter, aren't I!

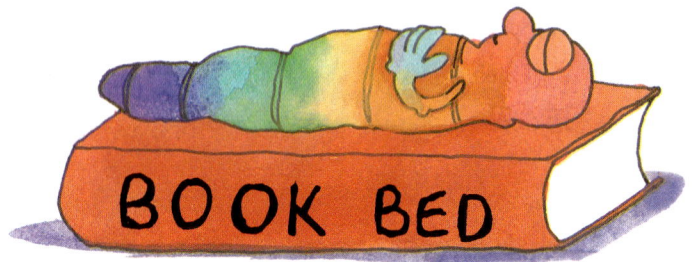

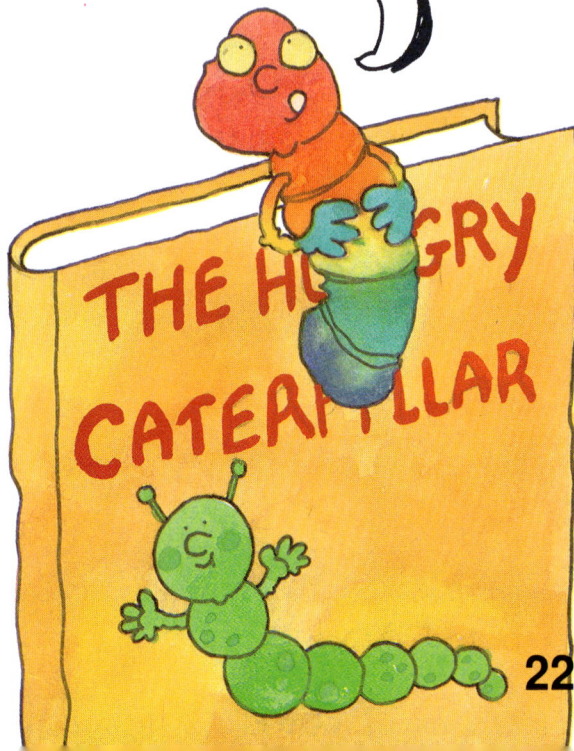

THE HUNGRY CATERPILLAR

Like my new hat?

22

Bookquiz

Here's a test to see if you have been concentrating on what we have told you about books in this book.

Try saying 'book quiz' 10 times very fast...

I already did, and I've turned into a b-b-b-blubbering wreck!

What is the biggest book ever printed?

What dotty pet did you see?

What is the smallest book ever printed?

Think of 3 things to describe the girl who is buying a book in the bookshop on page 20. Try not to cheat, though this can be very difficult.

What was the boy carrying on page 19?

What is another name for red?

How many fork-lift trucks were there on page 18?

Books!

There are different shapes and sizes, lengths and types of book made every day.

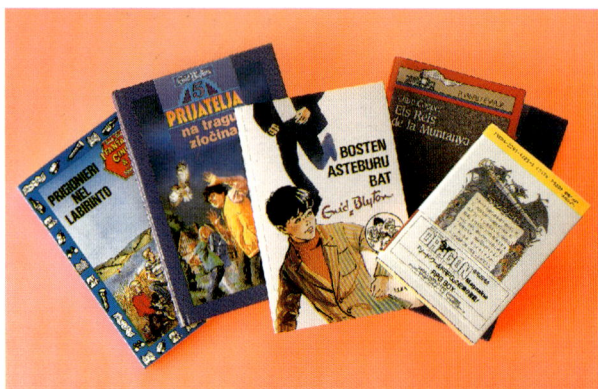

Representatives from publishing companies meet every year in different countries. These events are called book fairs, though there are no rides!

AMAZING FACTS!

The book that has been translated into the most languages is **The Bible**. It can be read in 314 languages.

Books!

If the publishers think people in their country would want to read a book they see at a fair, they will pay money to print it in their language. Some books have two languages printed on the same page.

In 1990, there were 63,980 different new books printed in the United Kingdom!

Once you have finished making your book from the card in the centre, try some more! Make books with things inside that are special for your family and friends, such as a photograph of a pet, a drawing of their teddy, or even a story about them.